First Generation Diesels in East Anglia

Alan C Butcher

ISBN 978-1-913251-04-8

First Published in 2020 by Transport Treasury Publishing Ltd, 16 Highworth Close, High Wycombe, HP13 7PJ.

www.ttpublishing.co.uk

Printed in the UK by Henry Ling Limited, at the Dorset Press, Dorchester, DT1 1HD.

Contents

Front cover: Brush Type 2 No. D5511 heads southwards through Saxmundham junction bound for London Liverpool Street. The first batch of the Brush Type 2 could easily be identified by the absence of train identification head code boxes, retaining the steam-era discs; albeit folding and supplemented by electric lighting for after dark train-type identification. *Dr Ian C Allen 086.*

Title page: A Derby Lightweight unit rolls southwards from Wells-Next-the-Sea towards Dereham, entering Ryburgh station as it does so. Serving the villages of Great Ryburgh (near the station) and Little Ryburgh (just to the north), the rail-connected maltings provided a useful source of originating traffic. Following closure to passenger traffic on 4th October 1969 the line remained open from Wymondham to Ryburgh for freight traffic until 1st August 1981. *Dr Ian C Allen D762.*

Opposite: Brush Type 2 No. D5572 at the head of a short freight, trundles along the Aldeburgh branch. When first opened by the Eastern Counties Railway on 12th April 1860 the name of the town was spelt Aldeborough. However, the GER amended the spelling to the more familiar version on 1st June 1875. *Dr Ian C Allen 523.*

Rear cover: With canal, road and rail alongside each other only one would win. Marriage's of Colchester and Felixstowe's Commer lorry could go places and travel further than a tramway locomotive governed to 12mph. Allocated to March depot for maintenance, the governors could be over-ridden when travelling away from the tramway, to their 25mph speed limit. This location is near Inglethorpe Hall, which stands behind the trees on the left. *Dr Ian C Allen 216.*

A note on the illustrations: All the illustrations in this book are from the Dr Ian C Allen collection now held by the Transport Treasury. The photographers notes available to the author often left a little to be desired – 'D5575 tn frt' – does not really help if the location cannot be identified. Bearing in mind also that over the last 60 years some places have changed out of all recognition. Few dates are given and of those some are suspect. Several locations were also wrongly named, hopefully the images used are now correctly identified. If you have any additional information or note something amiss, please contact the publisher so corrections can be made to future reprints.

Introduction

The eastern counties of England have a fascinating railway history. Much of the early history involves the Great Eastern Railway (GER), which either absorbed or built the majority of the network. Not having the heavy industry of some parts of the country, the lines were initially reliant on agricultural traffic. The opening up of the east coast ports to international trade stimulated traffic growth that is increasing still. Holiday traffic also helped the growth of the railways, Cromer and Hunstanton being just a couple of seaside destinations selected by those taking a break. Today Cromer still has its railway connection, whilst some in Hunstanton would like it back – if only to ease the journey to King's Lynn. Slightly further to the west, the residents of Wisbech are campaigning for a reopening of the line to March for passenger traffic.

The GER's monopoly was challenged to the north of Norwich by the Midland & Great Northern Joint Railway (M&GN) that ran west to east across Norfolk. Running across the country from Peterborough and Bourne, via South Lynn it reached Cromer, Great Yarmouth and Norwich. On the east coast the GER and M&GN co-operated by running the Norfolk & Suffolk Joint (N&SJt) lines from Lowestoft to Yarmouth and North Walsham to Cromer. Whilst the GER became part of the London & North Eastern Railway (LNER) at the grouping on 1st January 1923 the M&GN and N&SJt remained joint entities operated by the LNER and London, Midland & Scottish Railway (LMS) until Nationalisation.

Following the Nationalisation of the railways in 1948, the new owners – British Railways (BR) – began looking at what they now owned, the returns being made, and the investment required following World War 2. For a number of lines in Norfolk and Suffolk the figures did not look good. A study of *Atlas of Railway Station Closures* illustrates the routes closed to passenger traffic in the early 1950s. Virtually all the M&GN network was closed by the end of the decade.

Following the appointment of Dr Richard Beeching as Chairman, his report on the reshaping of the railway did not make for pleasant reading for those in Norfolk and Suffolk. Over half of the surviving passenger network lost its passenger services during the mid-1960s. In addition several routes earmarked for 'modernisation' – rationalisation was a better term – succumbed by the end of the decade. The cost cutting exercise had effectively cut too much and the limited services could not compete.

Although a number of lines remained open for general freight traffic, a lack of heavy or awkward loads meant that with the easier movement of goods by road, many had closed within a short period of time. With the demise of the railways, road improvements have obliterated the former track bed south of Great Yarmouth; and part of the A47 west from Dereham follows the route to King's Lynn.

The publication of this book just misses the anniversary of the closure of the M&GN, 60 years ago. At the same time, the first generation of main line diesels was being introduced, BR had yet to construct its last steam locomotive – No. 92220 *Evening Star*.

There are several instances of the railway and location not being referred to by the same name. As an example, although known generally as Great Yarmouth the name was not recognised by the railways until 16th May 1989; however, by this date only the former Vauxhall station was still operational. The

M&GN Beach station closed on 2nd March 1959 when most of the former joint line network was shut down. South Town station – actually in Southtown – survived until the closure of the southern section of the N&SJt route on 4th May 1970.

The section entries are not intended to be a full-blown history of the stretch of line or branch. At the back of the book is a Bibliography / Further Reading list that will, hopefully, satisfy those with a desire to learn more of an area that has an interesting and complex railway history.

Generally concentrating on Norfolk and Suffolk, where there is an interesting story to tell we will also step over the county boundaries. Indeed our journey starts just south of the River Stour at Harwich.

Despite Dr Beeching's best efforts it is still possible to travel over stretches of a main line network that is receiving investment. For those who wish to recall the past, the standard gauge heritage attractions – Mid-Norfolk Railway (GER) and North Norfolk Railway (M&GN), along with the 15in gauge Bure Valley Railway that runs along a former GER route, as does the 10.25in gauge Wells & Walsingham Railway; all operate timetabled services.

ACB, Dereham. 2019.

Almost straight 'out of the box' BTH Type 1 No. 8225 had only been in service for a few months when it was photographed at Earls Colne shunting the goods yard. Following cessation of passenger services the line remained opened for general freight traffic. Nearby was one of the first bases built by the United States in Britain following its involvement in World War 2. Becoming active in May 1943 service personnel and equipment would have passed through the station. *Dr Ian C Allen 260.*

1

Along the Essex Border

In July 1847 the Eastern Union Railway (EUR) was authorised to build a line from Manningtree heading east along the south bank of the River Stour to Harwich. The line opened on 15th August 1854. The route was slightly modified in 1882 when a loop added Parkeston Quay to the network with the original direct line closing the following year.

Above: Virtually at the very end of the line was the Harwich train ferry services to the continent commenced in April 1924, and continued until the last sailing on 31st January 1987. Here a 350hp shunter is propelling wagons on to one of the ferries that operated the service. In the late 1950s the *Essex Ferry*, *Norfolk Ferry* and *Suffolk Ferry* operated the Harwich–Hook of Holland service. The brake van was used as a 'spacer' wagon so that the locomotive did not cross the link span in use as a connection on to the vessel. The two tank wagons on the right would have contained fuel oil for the ferries. This was not the first location where the link span saw service. It was constructed in 1918 at Richborough Port in Kent, enabling military traffic direct rail access to Europe towards the end of World War 1; the first ferry left on 10th February, the final one towards the end of 1919. In 1922 the GER approached the Army to purchase the link span and three ferries; relocated to Harwich the facilities and ferries were to serve again during World War 2. *Dr Ian C Allen 323.*

Opposite top: Perhaps one of the most interesting of traffic movements in 1977, at least as far as the railway enthusiast was concerned, was the import of Class 56 locomotives that were built by Electroputere in Romania. Here two examples are being hauled from Harwich to Tinsley depot by a Brush Type 2, by now Class 31, for acceptance by BR. *Dr Ian C Allen 1001.*

At Mistley the quay was originally accessed by a line that descended down a 180° curve passing under the main line. In the early 20th century, the new line that was in use until 1991 replaced the original route. The Allied Breweries maltings are seen here with an unidentified 350hp shunter (later Class 08) passing on its way down to the riverside quays. *Dr Ian C Allen 004.*

Opposite top: Brush Type 2 (later Class 31) No. 5832 heads towards Mistley station with a freight service from Harwich. The 'Brighton Belle' motor coach was one of six Pullman Cars stabled in the sidings following purchase by Allied Breweries for use outside three of their public houses. The vehicles were Nos 285, 286 and 287 (Car Nos 85, 86 and 87) and Nos. 291, 292 and 293 (Car Nos 91, 92 and 93). Another Pullman Car will be seen at Sizewell later in our journey. There were plans for a railway running south – the Mistley, Thorpe & Walton Railway – authorised in July 1863; construction was abandoned in 1870. *Dr Ian C Allen 041.*

Opposite bottom: Having left the brake van on the access line to the quay as seen in the above image, an unidentified 350hp shunter is shunting a rake of grain-hoppers back into the storage siding just to the east of Mistley station which is visible through the bridge. This move was necessary as the road overbridge was not wide enough to allow for a traditional headshunt. The tall chimney carries the legend EDME Malt Extract Works. The food ingredient company has been in the village for 130 years, and at the time of writing its proposing to relocate is premises. *Dr Ian C Allen 1337.*

This page: English Electric Type 3 (later Class 37) No. 6734 passes through Manningtree on an Ipswich-London Liverpool Street service. The Eastern Union Railway originally opened the station on 15th June 1846; the building itself was rebuilt by the GER in 1899-1901 and still survives. The locomotives and rolling stock have been replaced several times since the 1950s, including electrification of the line, and at the time of writing, the latest upgrades are taking place. *Dr Ian C Allen 593.*

2

Colne Valley & Halstead Railway

The CV&HR was authorised in two stages. The first was for a line from Chappel & Wakes Colne station on the Colchester, Stour Valley, Sudbury & Halstead Railway to Halstead in June 1856. The second in August 1859 for an extension from Halstead to Haverhill, also on the CSV&HR. Close relations were maintained with the GER, however the CV&HR remained completely independent, until it became part of the LNER at the grouping in 1923.

Above: Wintertime at White Colne station. BTH Type 1 (later Class 15) No. D8228 awaits the next move as a member of the train crew strides purposefully past a box van body in use as a store. The guard has lit the fire in the brake van, note the smoke at the rear of the train. The line closed to passenger traffic from 1st January 1962. No. D8228 remained in traffic until March 1971 when it was withdrawn from service. These Type 1s were only intended for freight operation, but on a summer Saturday, could often be seen at the head of passenger workings. *Dr Ian C Allen 247.*

Opposite page: BTH Type 1 No. D8228 is seen at Halstead after passenger services were withdrawn. On what was now essentially a freight only line there was little need for signaling so BR removed the equipment and signal boxes. The original double track level crossing has been reduced to single, as evidence by the buffer stop adjacent to the crossing. General freight traffic ceased north of Halstead in 1964, the southern section finally closing on 19th April 1965. *Dr Ian C Allen 140.*

Opposite top: Further to the north BTH Type 1 No. D8215 is seen at the Haverhill end of Yeldham station shunting what is probably one of the final freight trains on this section. Actually located in Great Yeldham the station opened on 26th May 1862, closing to passengers on 1st January 1962. *Dr Ian C Allen 132.*

Opposite bottom: As we continue our journey along the CV&H, BTH Type 1 No. D8227 is seen approaching Birdbrook with a freight train in the early 1960s. The station here opened in 1863 and replaced a temporary one – Whitley – that had opened on 18th May 1863, only to close the following October.
No. D8227 was less than 10 years old when it was withdrawn in September 1968, barely outlasting the lines it was designed to work on. *Dr Ian C Allen 190.*

This page: A final view on the CV&H with an unidentified BTH Type 1 delivering the goods to Birdbrook. Economies dictated that a single signal post could do the job of two. No doubt the locomotive crew is thankful of a heated diesel cab, rather than an open cab steam locomotive. *Dr Ian C Allen 209.*

3

Stour Valley Railway

Authorised in June 1846 the Colchester, Stour Valley & Sudbury Railway ran from Marks Tey, on the EUR north to Sudbury. In 1847 an extension to Haverhill via Clare and Long Melford was authorised, along with a line northwards from Long Melford junction to Bury St. Edmunds on the Eastern Union Railway.

This page: One advantage of the first generation DMUs was their ability to haul tail loads, here a Cravens Class 105 two-car unit rolls in to Sudbury past Sudbury Goods Junction signal box on its way to Cambridge. Sudbury has had three stations over the years. The first opening with the railway in 1849, replaced when the line was extended to the north in 1865. This remained in use after the line closed in 1965 until relocated in 1990. *Dr Ian C Allen 249.*

Opposite top: The Derby Lightweight units were introduced into traffic in 1954. Here DMBS No. 79028 and DTCL No. 79617 form a Cambridge–Colchester service. Note the not uncommon use of a steam locomotive headlamp, looking as if it is just sitting on the buffer step plate. The goods yard that can be seen above the unit was the site of the original station, built in 1849 by the Great Eastern Railway. *Dr Ian C Allen 368.*

Opposite bottom: Another Derby Lightweight unit is seen at Sudbury during the course of its journey from Colchester. The circular item in front of the driver would be the carrier that holds the single line token authorising access to particular sections of track. As their name suggests the units were constructed using lightweight alloy sheets for body construction. This, and other non-standard features from later builds, resulted in their relatively short life span. *Dr Ian C Allen 530.*

This page: Long Melford was the junction for the Welnetham and Haverhill lines. Named Melford when opened in 1865 it gained its longer name on 1st February 1884. The Colchester-bound unit is a Derby Lightweight, with the Cambridge train a Class 109 built by D. Wickham & Co. There was a proposal in the early 20th Century to build the Long Melford & Hadleigh Light Railway between the two towns in the title. Although the Light Railway Order was granted the line was not built.   *Dr Ian C Allen 1372.*

Long Melford - Welnetham

Opposite: Following closure to passenger traffic in 1961 the line remained open to general freight traffic until 19th April 1965. BTH Type 1 No. D8225 is recorded at Lavenham as it waits to run round this short train. With the goods yard completely empty, and the BR delivery van parked up in this shot was probably taken just a few weeks before final closure. As usual following closure to passenger traffic the signaling has been removed, including the signalbox that was at this end of the platform, the foundations from which can be seen just behind the box van.   *Dr Ian C Allen 155.*

Opposite top: BTH Type 1 No. D8221 draws what appears to be a slightly more productive freight into Lavenham station; recorded on 14th April 1965 the end of freight services was less than a week away. The chalked note on the buffer beam 'The End' says it all. This is probably a clearance train removing all rolling stock from the line. Clearly visible is a white painted section on the over bridge. This enabled drivers to better read the signal position compared with a dark background. *Dr Ian C Allen 238.*

Opposite bottom: Further north the crew of No. D8221 pose on the platform at Welnetham. They would work the final train back to Bury St. Edmunds leaving the route to nature and the scrap men. *Dr Ian C Allen 110.*

This page: The same engine, BTH Type 1 No. D8221, propels a brake van out of the sidings at Cockfield. The station here had a single platform, on the down side of the line, with a single-storey rectangular brick building having a hipped slate roof. Opened as Cockfield, it was renamed Cockfield (Suffolk) on 1st October 1927 to avoid confusion with Cockfield in Durham, which was itself renamed Cockfield Fell in 1923. The goods yard handled a full range of goods traffic from the small yard opposite the platform; this comprised a single siding with a cattle dock. F. J. Jennings' private siding once ran from the yard to the adjacent Cockfield Hall, which was demolished in 1888. *Dr Ian C Allen 115.*

Above: Welnetham during the freight only era. The station here, along with Cockfield, had only a single platform. Located in the open countryside, most of the traffic would have been captured by road hauliers by this time. The yard here only handled a limited range of goods traffic with no facilities to handle livestock. This unidentified BTH Type 1 is heading northwards to Bury St. Edmunds. Welnetham closed to passengers on 10th April 1961 and to freight traffic on 13th June 1964. *Dr Ian C Allen 487.*

Long Melford - Haverhill

Opposite top: Seen just north of Long Melford this Sudbury-bound Derby Lightweight is seen at the site of the former junction of the Welnetham line. Long Melford station opened as Melford on 9th August 1865, and was renamed on 1st February 1884. The Welnetham line closed between here and Lavenham in 1961, and was subsequently lifted. The remaining section of line closed on 6th March 1967. *Dr Ian C Allen 529.*

Opposite bottom: This two-car Class 105 unit seen at Glemsford is another example of tail traffic as it heads in the direction of Cambridge. At the western end of the station was the coal yard, a couple of employees contemplate their next move, their delivery lorry hiding amongst the coal heaps. Around the turn of the 20th Century the nearest properties were a Mat Factory and an Inn. The trespass sign is of GER origin, and appears to be well and truly fixed to a length of rail. *Dr Ian C Allen 153.*

The station at Glemsford, with one of the four-wheel Waggon und Maschinenbau railbuses working to Colchester. Five vehicles were built in Germany in 1957, with the final vehicles surviving in traffic until 1967; their demise virtually coinciding with the branch they worked on. The station canopy now forms part of the replica building at Castle Hedingham station on the heritage Colne Valley Railway. *Dr Ian C Allen 103.*

With a tail load in tow, a two-car Class 105 Cravens unit is seen departing Glemsford for Haverhill. Note how the yard crew have protected the box vans they are loading with a baulk of timber placed across the track. The ability of the first-generation DMUs to handle tail loads was appreciated by the customers as it enabled parcels traffic to continue. With the demise of parcels traffic and wagonload freight the second-generation units were not fitted with conventional buffing gear. *Dr Ian C Allen 342.*

Brush Type 2 No. D5597 and 'J17' No. 65578 create a scene at Clare that was common during the modernisation era of the late 1950s and early 1960s. The small crane was hand-operated and a common sight around the goods yards. The station buildings and goods shed are still extant, as part of a visitor centre and museum for the Clare Castle & Country Park. It is interesting to note that the steam locomotive survived in traffic for more than twice that of the diesel. *Dr Ian C Allen 146.*

Opposite top: Haverhill with a Waggon und Maschinenbau railcar providing the service. To differentiate between the two stations in the town, North was added between 1923 and 1952. The CV&H station gained the suffix South, although the latter closed on 14th July 1924. The W&M railbuses were built in Germany, entering service in April 1958. On arrival in the UK window posters proclaimed 'Experimental railbus built by Mannheim (Brown Boveri of Switzerland)'. *Dr Ian C Allen 776.*

Opposite bottom: One of the Waggon und Maschinenbau railcars seemingly abandoned at Haverhill North and with a rake of carriages also stabled on the running line. Note the W. H. Smith sales outlet is closed - it must be a quiet Sunday afternoon! The five W&M railbuses were allocated to Cambridge and as delivered were painted in a light green livery with polished aluminium waist panel that went all round the vehicle. Add to that a light grey roof and they injected some colour into what was really a decaying system. *Dr Ian C Allen 389.*

This page: Depending on the final destination some services had to reverse at Bartlow Junction. Whilst Cambridge-bound services continued westwards, Audley End was to the southwest. This Waggon und Maschinenbau single car left the station and ran past the signalbox with the driver simply changing ends in order to continue the journey. The Bartlow–Audley End line closed to all traffic on 7th September 1964. *Dr Ian C Allen 932.*

4

Ipswich - Lowestoft

The route was built under several acts of Parliament. Initially the Eastern Union, built from East Suffolk Junction, Ipswich, to Woodbridge, opening in 1859. There with an end on junction, the East Suffolk Railway reached Lowestoft. The entire route became part of the GER in 1862.

Ipswich Docks.

Left: The docks at Ipswich straddled the River Orwell with the first references going back to the 8th Century. Development of the docks and associated infrastructure are on going and is under the ownership of Associated British Ports. To the north west of the station is the Upper Yard that gives access to the dock system. Standing in the yard are Drewry 204hp shunter (later Class 04) No. D2277 and a Brush Type 2, possibly No. 5566 that also appears to be carrying its Class 31 number, whilst a second shunter complete with runner goes about its duties. *Dr Ian C Allen 045.*

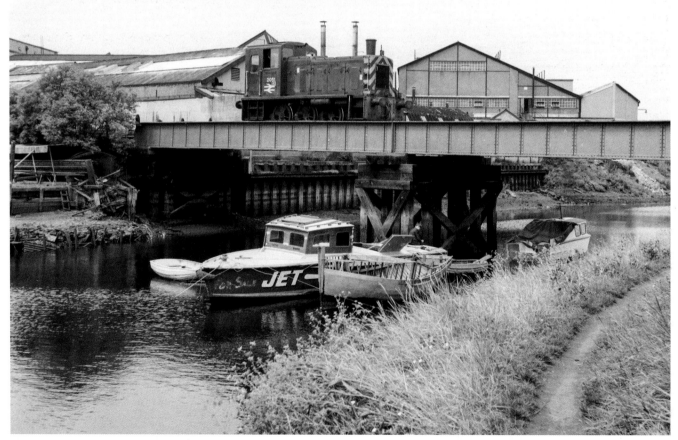

Opposite bottom: In order to gain access to the Lower Yard, also known as the goods station, the River Orwell had to be crossed. BR 204hp shunter (later Class 03) No. 2051 is seen on the bridge between the two yards. The young chap on the stern of 'Jet' seems more interested in the cameraman than the shunter. Following withdrawal in December 1972, No. 2051 survived scrapping and was sold to the Ford Motor Co at Dagenham. *Dr Ian C Allen 1317.*

This page, top: Brake van tours over goods only lines enabled a different view of proceedings, and access to generally restricted areas. The ILTS organised a dock tour on 24th August 1968, with Drewry shunter Nos. D2281 and D2282 sharing the duties. Note that both locomotives are fitted with cowcatchers and side skirts. No. D2281 has been specially cleaned for the occasion and the shed code – 32B (Ipswich) – has been painted on the buffer beam. The tour is seen here entering the Lower Yard on the north side of the River Orwell. *Dr Ian C Allen 1318.*

This page, bottom: The tour, being hauled by No. D2281 at this point, is heading towards the northern end of the line at Cliffe Road before returning to the Lower Yard. The tour, not being the usual fare, has caught the attention of the men working on their boat during low tide. *Dr Ian C Allen 050.*

Above; Returning to the main line, Westerfield is just north of Ipswich and the junction of the line to Felixstowe. Here Brush Type 2 No. 5851 is shunting a train of oil tankers. The shunter is hanging on to the brake van giving instructions to the driver. Two box vans are in use as barrier wagons. Of interest is the fine display of ground disc signals protecting the crossing and access to the sidings. Westerfield station was opened on 1st June 1859, and for a short period there was a second station; opened by the Felixstowe Railway on 1st May 1877 it closed on 1st September 1879. *Dr Ian C Allen 1151.*

Felixstowe

The story of the lines around Lowestoft is complex and readers are referred to '*Branch Lines to Felixstowe and Aldeburgh'* for the full story.

Opposite top: The Felixstowe Railway & Pier Co opened the line from Westerfield to Felixstowe Pier on 1st July 1877. A short branch to Felixstowe Town opened on 1st July 1898, with all traffic diverted to it, meaning all traffic for Beach station and the docks had to reverse here for the line south. Felixstowe Town lost its freight facilities in December 1966; however, the extensive track facilities were retained to provide storage capacity for the increasing dock traffic. The direct line to the by now extensive docks reopened in 1970 and with no need for such extensive sidings, the station layout was rationalized. A Brush Type 2 has run round a rake of wagons and as can be seen to the right of the image track lifting has commenced. Today a single platform remains in use for passenger traffic. *Dr Ian C Allen 733.*

Opposite bottom: Brush Type 2 No. D5652 heads over the 'new' West-South curve at Felixstowe shortly after reopening in 1970. The line to the town station via south to east curve was then abandoned and lifted, as there was no passenger traffic southwards. The trainload of containers was a sign of things to come as traditional wagon loads were beginning to lose out in favour of manufacture-to-customer deliveries. *Dr Ian C Allen D717.*

This page: Brush Type 2 No. 5518 and the former LNER Chief General Manager's saloon en route to Felixstowe docks passing the former east/south Junction. Of the two stations on this section of line, Pier closed on 2nd July 1951, with Beach closing on 11th September 1967. The current track layout allows the Felixstowe Dock & Railway Co two entrances to the docks to avoid conflicting train movements, one end being accessed from Trimley, the other through the site of the former Beach station. *Dr Ian C Allen D756.*

Opposite top: The Felixstowe Dock & Railway Co acquired a former BR Class 10 shunter, No. D3489, for shunting the docks, built at Doncaster in 1958; it was withdrawn by BR as being non-standard 10 years later. It was named *Colonel Tomline* by the FD&R after the man who was convinced that Felixstowe could be developed to rival Harwich on the other side of the Stour/Orwell estuary. Today, No. 3489 is on the Spa Valley Railway, one of the few locomotives illustrated to survive in preservation. *Dr Ian C Allen 278.*

Opposite bottom: English Electric Type 3 No. 6747 heads its short freight along the roadside tramway, effectively through the centre of an industrial estate as it returns to the main line at Trimley. Renumbered 37047 on 1st January 1973 it remained in service until August 2007. Initially allocated to Sheffield Darnall when new in 1962 it moved south to March in August 1967. *Dr Ian C Allen 621.*

Opposite top: Melton station was opened with the railway on 1st June 1857. Being located away from the village, falling passenger numbers meant that it was closed on 2nd May 1955. No. 5635 has shunted the coal yard at Melton and is departing with the empties. The goods yard would remain open until 1st June 1972, although it was retained as a private siding for domestic coal traffic and road stone between 1972 and 1976. After local campaigning the station reopened on 3rd September 1984. *Dr Ian C Allen 1357.*

Opposite bottom: The initial amount of investment in the East Suffolk line was considerable. The line north from East Suffolk Junction, Ipswich, to Halesworth, along with the Framlingham and Snape branches, all opened on 1st June 1859. Wickham Market station itself is situated in Campsea Ash, and No. D5576 is running past the lifted goods yard and sidings that closed in July 1964. *Dr Ian C Allen 1168.*

This page: Doyen of the English Electric Type 4s, No. D200 runs southbound through the station at Wickham Market. The first coach is of Bulleid build and is likely to one transferred to the Eastern Region from the Southern. On 16th April 1958 this locomotive undertook a demonstration trip between London Liverpool Street and Norwich, carrying a headboard proclaiming 'First 2,000hp diesel London-Norwich Progress by *Great Eastern*'. Allocated to Stratford depot when new it remained on the Eastern Region until May 1967 when it was transferred to the London Midland Region. Renumbered to 40122, it was condemned in April 1988 but subsequently preserved. *Dr Ian C Allen 186.*

Above: Just to the north of Wickham Market, BR/Sulzer Type 2 No. D5038 threads the scaffolding and netting that are in place to protect the railway from work taking place on the power lines passing overhead. The power cables originate at the Sizewell nuclear power station on the Aldeburgh branch. *Dr Ian C Allen 917*

Below and opposite top: The Framlingham branch was authorised in 1854; however, upon opening the branch and main line were promptly incorporated into the Eastern Counties Railway – the dominant company in East Anglia at the time. The branch closed to passenger services in November 1952, and to freight in April 1963. BTH Type 1 No. D8223 takes the Framlingham line at Wickham Market Junction with a single revenue earning mineral wagon a short time before closure. A few months later and the branch has been consigned to history as No. D5577 heads north. *Dr Ian C Allen 682 / 013*

Bottom: There was a short goods only line departing the main route at Snape Junction. This relatively unknown line, opened on the same day as the Ipswich-Halesworth route, operated weekdays only goods traffic. Though at times there could be as many as three trains a day as the maltings expanded. Prior to the arrival of the railway the malt and barley was generally exported through the port at Snape on the River Alde. Post World War 2 the maltings could not compete with the modern mechanised methods and rail traffic ceased on 4th March 1960. At Snape Junction a Cravens unit heads south to Ipswich, whilst an unidentified Class J15 waits to exit the branch with just a brake van in tow. *Dr Ian C Allen D415.*

Brush Type 2 No. 31114 is crossing between the running lines at Saxmundham. When opened on 1st June 1859 the platforms were staggered either side of the level crossing, and the other can just be seen behind the locomotive. With the increase in road traffic this was not acceptable and once the goods yard was closed it enabled a replacement platform for northbound services to be constructed in its place. For the second shot (below) Dr Allen has moved to the other side of the crossing and turned round. The Class 31 and an unidentified Class 47 are in charge of an engineering train seen under the canopy.
Dr Ian C Allen 300 / 614.

Saxmundham Junction

Top: Saxmundham junction was about half a mile north of the station. The double track continues north, whilst the Aldeburgh line rapidly becomes single. The signalman hands the single line token to the second man of Brush Type 2 No. D5566 as it heads a train of mineral wagons bound for Leiston and Aldeburgh. In 1972 the junction was simplified and Saxmundham Junction signal box taken out of service. *Dr Ian C Allen 482.*

Centre: A busy scene at Halesworth; the porter is probably loading products from the adjacent United Dairies factory on to the parcels train. A Brush Type 2 and train can be seen standing the other side of the road bridge. The BR/Sulzer Type 2 (later Class 24), No. D5042, is in charge of shunting the milk tankers, and having delivered the empties will be departing with a trainload of full ones. Note the road tanker being cleaned before refilling; with the second man, on the locomotive, offering the photographer a drink. Halesworth was the inland end of the 3ft gauge Southwold Railway, opening in 1879 it closed in 1929. *Dr Ian C Allen 513.*

Bottom: The ESR opened the section of line north from Halesworth to Haddiscoe on 4th December 1854, with the station at Brampton opened on the same day. As with the Halesworth-Ipswich section, this stretch was absorbed by the Eastern Counties Railway in 1859. To save confusion with a town of the same name – now in Cumbria – (Suffolk) was added to the station name on 1st June 1928. English Electric Type 4 (later Class 40) No. D201 heads south from Brampton. The class were introduced to the Great Eastern main lines in 1958, rapidly replacing steam on the main routes into East Anglia. Dr Allen's two-tone Austin Cambridge car is also seen parked by the crossing. *Dr Ian C Allen 1193.*

Opposite Top: An Ipswich bound Metropolitan-Cammell Lightweight unit stands at Brampton with a Norwich-Ipswich local service. Judging by the short stepladder against the lamppost the station was still gas lit at this time. *Dr Ian C Allen 215.*

Opposite bottom: This time it is an English Electric Type 3 at Brampton. As can clearly be seen the early members of the class had split head code boxes either side of the connecting doors. This view clearly shows the extremely heavy concrete posts that the GER used to hang level crossing gates from. *Dr Ian C Allen 742.*

Oulton Broad south to Lowestoft South Side

Bottom: The route from Beccles to Lowestoft opened, as with many lines at this time, on 1st June 1859. The station just to the west of the junction was originally named Carlton Colville, but it was renamed on 26th September 1927 to Oulton Broad South. An unidentified BR 204hp shunter makes its way from Lowestoft Harbour (also known as South Side) goods station across the junction. As it is effectively running 'wrong line' at this point it would continue the few yards into the down platform at Oulton Broad South where the locomotive would run-round its train. As there is a brake van at each end, this would only have taken a few minutes before continuing the journey to Lowestoft. *Dr Ian C Allen 019.*

This time it's a Brush Type 2, No. D5525, hauling a short train of box vans off the Lowestoft South Side branch. Driver and second man pose for Dr Allen. Allocated to Ipswich at this time, No. D5525 was to spend a period of time in the northeast before returning to East Anglia. It spent almost 50 years in service before withdrawal came in 2008. *Dr Ian C Allen 117.*

The route from the junction to the Harbour was between Kimberley Road, on the left, and the later development of Notley Road. A BR 204hp shunter makes its way from the harbour to the junction; the short freight has brake vans at both ends to make reversal at Oulton Broad station easier. The track is becoming overgrown indicating that maintenance has been allowed to drift and closure is not that far away. *Dr Ian C Allen 021.*

Just over a mile from the junction the line divided into three: to Kirkley Goods Depot, South Side and Machonochie Brothers Ltd. The latter was a family firm that was largely responsible for the development of the town. The junction was intersected by Durban Road level crossing, and a flagman duly protects the train as it crosses the road shortly before closure. The Kirkley line closed in 1966 and was subsequently lifted, the wagons are standing on the line to South Side, which leaves the Class 03 departing with traffic from the Machonochie factory siding. *Dr Ian C Allen 147.*

This page: A BR 204hp shunter rolls back over the level crossing to collect a rake of oil tankers. The shunter – probably also acting as flagman – can be seen just to the left of the locomotive. As mentioned in the previous caption the line to Kirkley Goods has been closed and lifted; the South Side connection has now suffered the same fate. *Dr Ian C Allen 157.*

Opposite top: The oil tankers in the previous view would have come from the Co-Operative Wholesale Society Ltd's canning factory. With a load of tarpaulined wagons in tow, the flagman is escorting the BR shunter across the network of nearby roads. *Dr Ian C Allen 134.*

Opposite bottom: When Dr Allen returned at a later date, he photographed BR shunter No. D2034 on the Durban Road level crossing from the other side. The wagons beyond the brake van are specialist wagons built for the carriage of timber and would have been ideal for the Boulton & Paul traffic. *Dr Ian C Allen 311.*

Above: Different motive power this time in the shape of a Hunslet 204hp, later Class 05 shunter. The flagman escorts No. D2563 alongside the road. The locomotive was withdrawn from traffic in January 1968, a matter of weeks after the final closure by BR of the South Side network. *Dr Ian C Allen 835.*

Opposite top: Following closure Boulton & Paul retained a section of line as a private siding and operated their own Baguley diesel shunter (works No. 3509/1958) that was transferred to their Norwich operation when the line closed on 31st December 1972. Here it and BR 204hp shunter No. D2035 stand in the works yard during the final years. Boulton & Paul were known for the furniture they built and their woodworking skills were put to good use in the Defiant aircraft that flew for the RAF during World War 2. *Dr Ian C Allen 1270.*

Opposite bottom: No. D2039 goes about its duties shunting the Boulton & Paul yard. The sheeted wagons have been loaded and await being tripped to the yards north of the river, via Oulton Broad South. The specialist wood-carrying wagons can be seen to better effect in this image. *Dr Ian C Allen 723.*

5

Haddiscoe

Haddiscoe was at the heart of a railway crossroads; it was named after the village of Haddiscoe, some two miles distant, although the village of St Olaves on the other side of the River Waveney is closer.

An earlier Haddiscoe station was opened by the Norfolk Railway on 1st July 1847 but was later closed by the GER on 9th May 1904. It was replaced by the current station, opened on 9th May 1904, and originally named Haddiscoe Low Level, at the junction of the Reedham–Somerleyton route and the now closed Yarmouth-Beccles line from London to Yarmouth. An existing station on the Yarmouth-Beccles Line at this junction was renamed from Herringfleet Junction to Haddiscoe High Level at the same time. Both the High Level station and the Low Level station operated until the British Transport Commission withdrew services on the Yarmouth line in 1959 and closed the associated High Level station. BR subsequently renamed the remaining station Haddiscoe. A link between the two lines existed, controlled by Haddiscoe Junction signal box. A Brush Type 2 is at the head of a sugar beet working at Haddiscoe low level station; Fleet Junction is behind the train. *Dr Ian C Allen 201.*

6

Framlingham Branch

The Framlingham branch started from a junction at Wickham Market station and was officially opened on 1st June 1859. However, the East Suffolk Railway was promptly incorporated into the Eastern Counties Railway, the dominant railway company in East Anglia at this time.

BR/Sulzer Type 2 No. D5041 with a lone brake van in tow makes its leisurely way along the branch. It was always winter when Dr Allen visited the line, but this was probably the only time when freight traffic, in the form of coal, could be almost guaranteed. Framlingham station dealt with significant goods traffic until the 1950s and also had a small single tracked engine shed where the branch steam locomotive was kept overnight. *Dr Ian C Allen 1034.*

Higher authority was looking the other way when this shot at Marlesford was recorded. As BR/Sulzer Type 2 No. D5040 and train traverse the level crossing a member of the train crew appears to be conversing with the driver. There were no goods facilities here; and the train crew would have been responsible for opening and closing the crossing gates. *Dr Ian C Allen 152.*

Opposite top: With three empty mineral wagons, box and brake van in tow, No. D8220 was not earning much revenue for BR on this trip. No. D8220 entered service in March 1960 and was initially allocated to Stratford. During its time working on the branch it would have been allocated to Ipswich. Having spent its working life in East Anglia it was one of the members of the class to survive until the very end, being withdrawn on 27th March 1971 from Stratford depot. *Dr Ian C Allen 400*

Opposite bottom: The station yard appears to have been taken over by the local coal merchant as passenger services ceased on 3rd November 1952. By the early 1960s most of the traffic would have been in coal as this was then still the staple fuel for heating homes. The driver of No. D8221 looks back towards the photographer – or perhaps the shunter – before making his next move. *Dr Ian C Allen 251.*

This page: No. D8220 awaits departure from Framlingham with two empty wagons and brake van in tow. Although the branch closed to passenger traffic on 3rd November 1952, the general platform area looks reasonably well kept as the occasional school specials ran. The line remained open for freight traffic until April 1963. *Dr Ian C Allen 178.*

7

Aldeburgh Branch

The East Suffolk Railway had opened a branch line between Saxmundham and Leiston predominantly to serve Garrett's engineering works on 1st June 1859. The town of Aldeburgh had lobbied hard and

permission to extend the branch was granted on 19th April 1859. The Eastern Counties Railway that had taken over the operation of the East Suffolk Railway built the line.

With RAF Leiston about a mile from the town and the engineering works of Garrett making munitions, the town itself would have been a busy place during the latter years of World War 2. A decade or so later Brush Type 2 No. D5679 rolls into Leiston from the west with a well wagon and a couple of loaded coal wagons in tow. The sidings seen here were a later addition added when traffic on the branch increased. To the right of the image one of the utility companies is laying pipes along the road. *Dr Ian C Allen 268.*

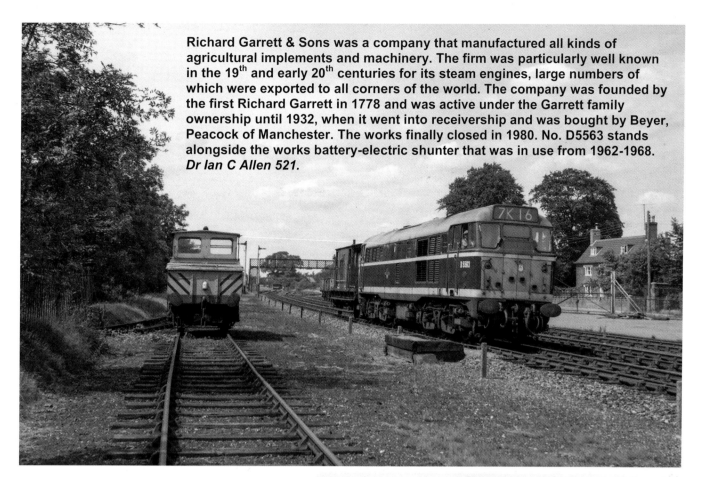

Richard Garrett & Sons was a company that manufactured all kinds of agricultural implements and machinery. The firm was particularly well known in the 19th and early 20th centuries for its steam engines, large numbers of which were exported to all corners of the world. The company was founded by the first Richard Garrett in 1778 and was active under the Garrett family ownership until 1932, when it went into receivership and was bought by Beyer, Peacock of Manchester. The works finally closed in 1980. No. D5563 stands alongside the works battery-electric shunter that was in use from 1962-1968. *Dr Ian C Allen 521.*

Right: Not a view to be expected on a quiet branch line as a Brush Type 2 prepares to collect two whitewashed coaches that have been used as part of a fire and rescue training exercise, probably in connection with the nuclear facility at Sizewell. The coaches are former LMS vehicles; the nearer being a post 1933 Stanier-designed steel-sided coach with the second dating from the 1929-1933 period. Just visible to the left of the shunter is a father and son, safe in the knowledge that a set of buffer stops is barring rail access to the former goods shed. *Dr Ian C Allen 800.*

Bottom: With the Royal Train head code being carried, and once painted white buffers, No. 5526 has, seemingly, fallen on hard times as it heads a train past Leiston station following lifting of all but the running line through the station. With the level crossing gates closed against the train just ahead, a member of the crew will need to open them before the driver can progress. It is recorded that the locomotive hauled the Royal Train conveying HM Queen Elizabeth from King's Cross to Peterborough on 27th March 1975, although at that time the locomotive was numbered 31108. *Dr Ian C Allen 179.*

This page: DMU services commenced in June 1956. An Ipswich bound Metropolitan-Cammell lightweight unit heads away from Leiston as a member of the station staff returns to his office duties and a passenger strides purposefully along the platform. *Dr Ian C Allen 772.*

Opposite top: BTH Type 1 No. D8236 has arrived with a civil engineers' crane in tow; something needed lifting but Dr Allen appears not to have recorded the facts. Grafton built the crane, No. 330520, in 1939; with a 10-ton capacity it remained in service until 1982. The lines curving away to the right lead to Garrett's engineering works. Behind the battery-electric locomotive there is a raised platform used for loading wheeled vehicles on to railway wagons, hence the need for the loading gauge seen above the locomotive. The battery-electric locomotive was built in 1927 by Electromobile (works No. S247) of Otley, Yorkshire. Electromobile was one of the first firms to build battery-electric locomotives for industrial use. Delivered new to Shoeburyness it was used by the War Department. Photographs published in *Railway Bylines* (Vol 4 No. 11) show it attached to an armoured wagon in early 1941 – the locomotive was wooden-bodied! *Dr Ian C Allen 051.*

Opposite bottom: Brush Type 2 No. D5528 heads an empty coal train back to the main line. The wagon on the line to Garrett's has a farm implement for a load. *Dr Ian C Allen 1370.*

BR/Sulzer Type 2 No. D5040 appears to still be on coal train duties, although this time with a box van added to the consist as it slowly passes through the station. There is a low-sided wagon parked in the loop destined for Garretts works and to the right of Dr Allen a grain hopper, an unusual visitor to the branch. The concrete blocks are 'stools' for burying in the ground to support point rodding and signal wires, presumably left over from when some Signalling & Telegraph work was undertaken.
Dr Ian C Allen 515.

Gas works.

An unidentified Brush Type 2 stands at the entrance to Leiston Gas Works just to the east of the station. The works were owned by Messrs Richard Garrett & Sons and lit 40 public street lamps as well as supplying gas for domestic use. Along with a gas supply the company also supplied water to the town from its Works well, until a public supply was installed just before World War 1. In the adjacent yard is a Moy's lorry. The Thomas Moy company was well known as coal merchants and had its own private owner coal wagon fleet.
Dr Ian C Allen 200.

Brush Type 2 No. D5525 at the head of a track recovery train following closure of the line south of Sizewell. When BR decided to dismantle the line using direct labour they had access to better kit than independent scrap dealers. They did not have to hire wagons to take the track away for recycling. The runner wagon behind the locomotive will protect it in case the load shifts on the wagons, important as the track panels do not appear to be strapped down.   *Dr Ian C Allen 079.*

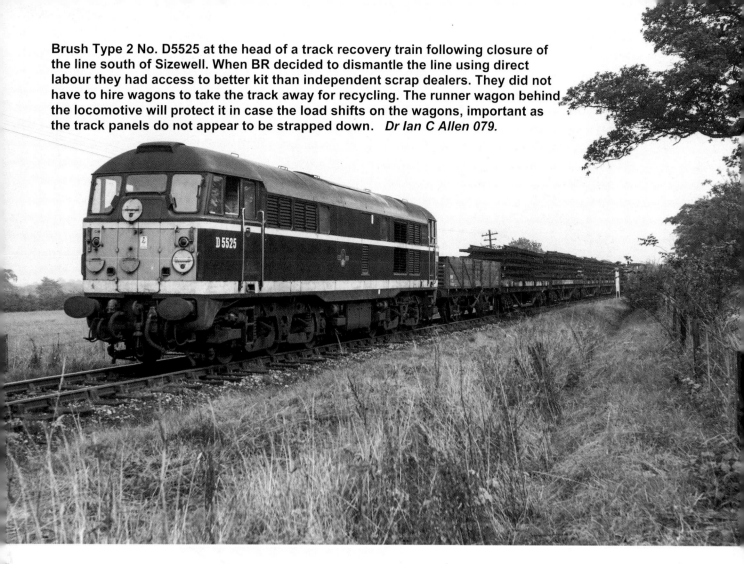

BR/Sulzer Type 2 No. D5040 heads an empty coal train from Aldeburgh towards Leiston. A number of the class were allocated to the Eastern Region from new and No. D5040 was sent to Ipswich when delivered in October 1959, moving to March a few weeks later then back to Ipswich in June 1960.
Dr Ian C Allen 102.

Class 37 No. 37114 and brake van make their way along the line between Sizewell and Leiston. The bridge shown here was the only major engineering structure on the line and carried the railway over Valley Road on the outskirts of Leiston. The locomotive spent most of its working life allocated to March depot and would have been a regular visitor to East Anglian lines. *Dr Ian C Allen 358.*

Brush Type 2 No. 5566 pulls a single loaded flask wagon back over the road as the second man and driver look forward checking that the crossing is clear. The flasks are used to transfer fuel or radioactive waste to the reprocessing plant at Sellafield, although, at this date, the latter was known as Windscale. *Dr Ian C Allen 325.*

For safety reasons the transfer of nuclear flasks takes place away from the power station itself. The first reference for Sizewell Crossing is in 1879 when a local landowner asked for the siding to be 'put in order'. Eighty years later it was to become the site of the transfer point for the nearby Sizewell nuclear power station. The driver of BTH Type 1 No. D8223 looks back, awaiting the next instruction from the shunter standing by the crossing. An empty flask wagon can be seen standing in the adjacent siding. The large gantry crane was installed in the early 1960s. *Dr Ian C Allen 816.*

Not what you expect to see on the doorsteps of a nuclear power station. Upon withdrawal 'Brighton Belle' Car No. 284 was privately preserved at Westleton, Suffolk. Hauled by Brush Type 2 No 5550, the first part of the journey was by rail to Sizewell, thence for onward transportation by road. In April 1985 Sea Containers Ltd acquired it for restoration. Today 'Vera' regularly runs on the main line as part of the 'Belmond British Pullman' consist. *Dr Ian C Allen 1198.*

The driver of the Brush Type 2 awaits instructions from the shunter, hidden by a leg of the gantry crane, as he uncouples a wagon. The use of 'runner' wagons, in this case a mineral wagon, was common if the locomotive was hauling a hazardous load. *Dr Ian C Allen 685.*

The Class 37 at the current end of the line, with a flask loaded on the wagon - again the driver looks back awaiting his next instruction. Today services to transport nuclear flask trains are provided by Direct Rail Services from their depots at Crewe and Carlisle. At the time of writing Sizewell C power station is under consideration, one of the options being to use the existing line for construction traffic.

This page: Metropolitan-Cammell lightweight unit No. 79281 leads the way to Ipswich, at Thorpness. Seemingly in the middle of nowhere the station was not opened until 29th July 1914, with just a single line platform and rudimentary facilities. In later years two additional coach bodies were added to improve the facilities. These did not stand directly on the platform, but on concrete supports. What intending passengers thought of the station comforts is best left to the imagination. With this section of the line reduced to 'pay train' status, the guard was responsible for the opening and closing of the level crossing gates. *Dr Ian C Allen 083 / 517.*

Aldeburgh was home to the composer Benjamin Britten and has been the centre of the international Aldeburgh Festival of Arts at nearby Snape Maltings, founded by Britten in 1948. Metropolitan-Cammell lightweight unit No. 79282, nearest the camera, awaits departure time. By this time the section south from Leiston was operated as 'one train in section' and all signalling had been removed. The weed-strewn run round loop signifies that the end is near, with the station canopy removed during the summer of 1965; closure came on 12th September 1966. *Dr Ian C Allen 516.*

8

Ipswich - Norwich

The main line from London (Liverpool Street) to Norwich was built northwards from Ipswich by the Ipswich & Burt St. Edmunds Railway, with the line opening on 24th December 1846. Seven months later, on 9th July 1847, the company was absorbed into the Eastern Union Railway. The Haughley to Norwich section was opened by the Eastern Union on 12th December 1849.

Opposite top: Track work in hand at Haughley level crossing with Brush Type 2 No. D5695 at the head of a ballast train. Haughley station itself closed on 2nd January 1967 as part of the Beeching Axe and, as can be seen, most of the station building was demolished as well as the three platforms and the two signal boxes, the turntable pit filled in and the sidings removed. By now high-visibility vests are in evidence. *Dr Ian C Allen 327.*

Just to the north of the former Haughley station, Brush Type 2 No. 5800 heads a short train consisting of a civil engineering crane and five hoppers, mineral wagon and a couple of brake vans. There was once a short-lived Haughley Road station that was operational from 24th December 1846 to 9th July 1849, it was situated about a mile along the line towards Burt St. Edmunds. *Dr Ian C Allen.*

Haughley Junction.

Above: Haughley was once a three-way junction; the line westward to Burt St. Edmunds and Newmarket remains operational as does the line northwards to Norwich. The line eastwards was the connection to the Mid-Suffolk Light Railway (MSL). A late arrival on the railway scene, passenger services on the MSL reached Laxfield on 29th September 1908. A planned extension towards Halesworth was never completed. The MSL was closed in its entirety on 28th July 1952. BR/Sulzer Type 2 (Class 25) No. D7588 passes the site of the MSL junction. *Dr Ian C Allen 930.*

Opposite top: This time viewed from the west of the line as Brush Type 2 No. D5693 heads a trainload of three mineral wagons and a few flat wagons containing farm implements. Today the junction has been simplified with a single connection to the Burt St. Edmunds line and a cross over between the main line tracks. *Dr Ian C Allen 339.*

Opposite bottom: Courtesy of a friendly signalman this shot was taken from the 'box at Haughley Junction. The track of the Mid-Suffolk Railway is still intact at this time as Brush Type 2 No. D5507 heads south. Whilst the majority of the train is made up from BR Mark 1 coaches in 'blood and custard' livery the leading vehicle is a Gresley corridor carriage, dating from the 1930s. The carriage retains its BR maroon livery; with the vast majority of these vehicles being withdrawn by the close of 1964. *Dr Ian C Allen 265.*

Mellis Junction was where the Eye branch left the main line. The Mellis & Eye Railway opened the line to Eye on 2nd April 1867. Running between the two locations mentioned in the title, there were no intermediate stations although ultimately a halt was built at Yaxley opening on 2nd December 1922. The line closed to passengers on 2nd February 1932, remaining open for general freight traffic until 1964. Brush Type 2

No. D5828 is seen at the junction itself, with the by now closed and lifted line to Eye curving away to the right. Mellis station closed on 7th November 1966. *Dr Ian C Allen 1329.*

The station at Diss was proposed by the Ipswich & Bury Railway as part of their route to Norwich. The Ipswich & Bury Railway was taken over by the Eastern Union Railway, which started operating in 1849. This became part of the Eastern Counties Railway (ECR) in 1854, which amalgamated with several other companies in 1862 to form the GER. Class 31 No. 31123 is in the goods yard at Diss. The line gave access to the grain silos that can be seen. It is reported that horses carried out some wagon shunting here as late as 1959. *Dr Ian C Allen 044.*

Heading towards Norwich, BTH Type 1 Nos. D8222 and D8226 double-head a freight train out of Diss in 1968. Both the locomotives led similar lives, allocated to the Eastern Region when new and spent all their lifes there. Both were withdrawn from Stratford depot on 27th March 1971, the last day in service for any member of the class, they were subsequently cut up at Crewe Locomotive Works. *Dr Ian C Allen 228.*

Allocated to Norwich Thorpe when new, Hunslet 204hp shunter No. 11168 heads a special across Trowse Upper Junction, on 31st March 1962. This was part of the Great Eastern Commemorative Steam Rail Tour that was run by the RCTS. This tour was organised to celebrate the passing of steam haulage on the Great Eastern main line. BR Standard Class 7 No. 700033 *John Bunyan* hauled the train to Norwich Victoria from London Liverpool Street. No. 11168 then hauled the train back to Trowse Upper Yard from where it continued to Norwich Thorpe. Norwich Victoria closed to passenger traffic on 22nd May 1916, but remained open for goods traffic until 1966. No. 11168 was renumbered D2565 in March 1963 and withdrawn in
March 1967. *Dr Ian C Allen 105.*

BR 204hp shunter No. D2035 hauls empty coaching stock across Norwich Thorpe Junction on the way to the station. The current Norwich Thorpe station is the second on the site. The original being replaced by the current one in 1886, it remained in use until the 1980s as part of the goods station. The locomotive is in as delivered livery with no yellow and black chevrons to disfigure it. The area behind the signal box is part of Crown Point depot that has recently been upgraded for the new units in the course of delivery. *Dr Ian C Allen 236.*

9

Waveney Valley

The Waveney Valley line was a branch line running from Tivetshall in Norfolk to Beccles in Suffolk connecting the Great Eastern Main Line at Tivetshall with the East Suffolk line at Beccles. It provided services to Norwich, Great Yarmouth, Lowestoft, Ipswich and many other smaller towns in Suffolk with additional services to London. It was named after the River Waveney whose course it follows.

An unidentified Hunslet 204hp shunter is seen at the closed Geldeston station, the first stop out of Beccles. The station opened to traffic with the opening of the line on 2nd March 1863. It closed briefly between 22nd May and 14th September 1916. Finally closing to passengers on 5th January 1953, and completely on 13th July 1964. A member of the train crew is alighting to open the level crossing gates at the Beccles end of the station. *Dr Ian C Allen 430*.

Opposite top: With the former Ellingham station just behind the train, the platform can be seen just beyond the crossing gates. BR 204hp shunter No. D2034 heads towards Beccles. Along with Geldeston the station suffered a period of closure, from 22nd May 1916, but this time not reopening until 1st August 1919. Road improvement has meant that much of the Waveney Valley route is now under tarmac.
Dr Ian C Allen 1227.

Opposite bottom: Hunslet 204hp shunter No. D2559 and train crossing the Norwich Road at Ditchingham bound for Beccles. General freight services ceased on 19th April 1965, but the Ellingham sand traffic kept the line open for a few more months. The unusual 16 ton mineral wagons, seen here, originated in the early 1940s for use in France after D-Day and were returned to BR in the 1950s. Once this traffic ended the line passed into history. The maltings here were the mainstay of the final freight traffic, as well as employing hundreds of local people working seven days a week for eight months a year as maltsters; the buildings had also been used by American servicemen during World War 2. While happy with their posting making great friends with the welcoming local community, they also started a 'Friendship Wall' inscribing their name and the US State they called home on to one of the walls inside the maltings.
Dr Ian C Allen 971.

This page: Near Starston a Brush Type 2 heads a freight train through the countryside. Starston station had a short life, opening on 1st December 1855, it closed 10 years later on 1st August 1866. Following closure to passenger traffic on 5th January 1953 the line between Harleston and Tivetshall remained open for general freight services until 18th April 1966. The central section of the line from Harleston to Ditchingham closed to freight traffic on 1st February 1960. *Dr Ian C Allen 222.*

10

Norwich - Yarmouth

The Yarmouth & Norwich Railway (Y&N) opened the route between the two towns, via Reedham and Brundall, on 1st May 1844. The line's eastern terminus opened as Yarmouth Vauxhall, becoming just Yarmouth when the town's two other stations closed. Finally BR adopted the town's name for the station – Great Yarmouth – on 16th May 1989.

Reedham junction is the second of two on the Norwich-Yarmouth line where the line splits for Yarmouth and Lowestoft. Reedham station opened with the line and was, as it is now, situated east of Cantley station and west of Berney Arms. The Y&N was the first public railway line in Norfolk. On 1st July 1847 the Norfolk Railway opened the Lowestoft to Reedham line. The station southeast of Reedham on the line to Lowestoft was Haddiscoe. Having called at Reedham station, this Yarmouth bound DMU is approaching the junction itself. *Dr Ian C Allen D1545.*

Yarmouth Quay

The quay was accessed by both the GER (from Vauxhall station) and the M&GN from Caister Road
Junction on the NS&Jt line to Beach station. The latter had a yard at White Swan – named after a local inn
– where there was an end-on connection with the GER line. Following closure of the M&GN in 1959 the
GER route was the only means of access. The lines to the quays were worked by tramway locomotives
that were kept at the GER engine shed at Vauxhall station when not in use. The steam, then diesel
locomotives clattered their way through the streets of Yarmouth for many decades and during the final
years were frequently held up by cars parked across the lines. The lines were finally abandoned during the
1970s.

A 204hp shunter pulls in off the quayside tramway with a rake of mineral wagons in tow. Swan Yard coal
depot was protected by a set of gates, which the flagman will have opened for the train to pass through
the 'hole in the wall', alongside the White Swan public house. The tower is part of the town wall built
around the turn of the 13th and 14th centuries, and now a scheduled ancient monument. The town wall
had 11 towers along its length, forming part of the defensive 'flinty ring of steel'. *Dr Ian C Allen 822*

Opposite page, top: With weeds rapidly taking hold following closure of the M&GN route to the quayside seen behind the locomotive, No. D2032 is at the Ormond Road end of Swan Yard. The coal siding in the yard was laid in the early 1900s and by 1908 was operated by the Great Yarmouth Co-Operative Society. *Dr Ian C Allen 022.*

Opposite page, bottom: The North Tower dominates the skyline in this view as the shunter treads carefully as he goes about his duties in Swan yard. The narrow space between the White Swan and adjacent building was known as the 'hole in the wall'. *Dr Ian C Allen 171.*

This page: A flagman protects the train as it leaves Swan yard heading towards North Quay junction. Under the Rules & Regulations for operating the tramway it was noted that the gates to the yard, seen behind the train, had to be secured against public access before shunting could commence. The yard was finally closed in May 1970. *Dr Ian C Allen 539.*

Above: Following closure of the M&GN, access to the quay was via the GER's bridge across the River Bure. Drewry 204hp shunter No. D2210 has just crossed the bridge heading for North Quay junction. The bridge was available for road access to the station. Road access to the town was eased with the opening of the Acle New Road (A149) that bridged the River Bure slightly to the north of the original crossing point. *Dr Ian C Allen 434.*

Opposite top: BR 204hp shunter No. D2032 running along the roadside at North Quay junction. Not all the shunters that worked on the quayside line had the cowcatchers and side skirts that the unidentified Drewry shunter in the second view carries. *Dr Ian C Allen 558.*

Opposite bottom: During the later years when the line was less intensively used there are tales of parked vehicles being man-handled clear of the tracks here the flag man does not look amused at the Morris Traveller blocking his path. Jewsons, whose yard can be seen above the train in the first illustration, opened its first branch in 1836. *Dr Ian C Allen 151.*

An all too familiar sight during the 1960s as Drewry shunter No. D2210 hauls a trainload of scrap rails along the quayside at Hall Quay. Here the quayside line has its own dedicated right of way.
The shunter does not have to clear pedestrians and cars out of the way here, so he has hitched a lift.
Haven Bridge – or Southtown Bridge – can be seen to the left of the locomotive. The bridge spanning the River Yare is constructed from cast iron supported by stone bascules with cast iron railings; it was opened in 1930. *Dr Ian C Allen 177.*

11

Wroxham - Aylsham - Lenwade

At one time it was possible to take a day trip from Norwich and return there without changing trains – or indeed reversing direction. Norwich–Wroxham–Aylsham–County School–Dereham–Wymondham–Norwich, or the reverse was possible.

Northbound from Norwich and with North Walsham as its destination, this Metropolitan-Cammell unit is about to reach the junction for the former East Norfolk Railway's Aylsham–County School line at Wroxham. This view being taken from the signalbox; looking towards the station. Opened as Wroxham on 20th October 1874, the station was renamed Hoveton & Wroxham on 12th May 1960. The Aylsham route closed to passenger traffic on 15th September 1952 and to general freight on 1st March 1977. *Dr Ian C Allen 016.*

Coltishall goods yard, with signage of No Admittance, No Smoking and Danger, to satisfy Health & Safety requirements. A temporary loading facility was in use here for the loading of condensate from Bacton gas terminal until the completion of a dedicated loading facility at North Walsham. Brush Type 2 No. D5657 and runner wagon are in attendance. Trains still run through the station site, albeit in the form of the 15in gauge Bure Valley Railway that opened in July 1990. *Dr Ian C Allen 889.*

From 1957 Lenwade was the location of important concrete works, one of the main products being large beams for use in motorway bridge construction. The safest way at the time to transport these was by rail. With its location on the former M&GN line into Norwich, the only way out was to transport the beams via a roundabout route, Melton Constable–Cromer avoiding line–North Walsham and on to Norwich. To shorten journey time a curve was constructed between the former M&GN and GER lines at Themelthorpe. The curve was the final section of new standard gauge track opened in Norfolk in the 20th Century. The line closed on 15th June 1983, being lifted the following year.

Above: English Electric Type 3 No. 6726 is seen on the Themelthorpe curve bound for Lenwade. No. 6726 was one of the early class members and carries its split head code boxes either side of connecting doors. Early diesels had end doors that enabled the crew to access a second locomotive when double heading. A source of draughts in the cab, they were not liked by the crews and later builds did not have them. *Dr Ian C Allen 028.*

Opposite top: Lenwade station was built by the Lynn & Fakenham Railway, opening on 1st July 1882 and taken over by the Midland & Great Northern Joint Railway in 1893, to serve the small hamlet of Lenwade. Despite the settlement's size, the railway provided a direct service to Norwich and King's Lynn. It closed to passengers on 28th February 1959, but remained open to goods trains until 1983. An unidentified BR 204hp shunter is passing by Lenwade station, the driver checking that all is well. *Dr Ian C Allen 126.*

Opposite bottom: Another load of pre-cast concrete beams leave Lenwade concrete works, this time a Brush Type 2 is in charge. Note the concrete signal post, this would have originated from the M&GN's works at Melton Constable. The M&GN under the auspices of their engineer Mr Marriott was an early manufacturer of concrete products – signal posts, gateposts, station name boards and fence posts just a small selection of the output. *Dr Ian C Allen 505.*

12

M&GN and N&SJt.

The Midland & Great Northern Joint Railway (M&GN) connected southern Lincolnshire and north Norfolk. It developed from several local independent concerns and was incorporated in 1893. The Midland Railway and the Great Northern Railway jointly owned it; those companies had long sponsored and operated the predecessor companies. The area directly served was agricultural and sparsely populated; but seaside holidays had developed and the M&GN ran many long distance express trains to and from the territory of the parent companies, as well as summer local trains for holidaymakers. It had the longest mileage of any joint railway in the United Kingdom.

Above: As the M&GN line approached Cromer from the west, following the coastal cliff tops, it avoided the steep escarpment that had prevented the earlier GER line from Norwich running all the way into the town. Consequently, it became possible to build a far more conveniently located station, near to the town centre and the beach. The station opened as Cromer Beach on 16th June 1887 and was renamed Cromer on 20th October 1969, following the closure the GER's Cromer High station on 20th September 1954. A connecting line linking the GER and M&GN lines had opened in 1906. Here a Cravens Class 105 set is seen departing Cromer. *Dr Ian C Allen D812.*

Opposite top: Notwithstanding its rural location, Melton Constable station became an important railway centre with lines converging from all directions providing connections to key East Anglian towns such as King's Lynn, Norwich, Cromer, Fakenham and Yarmouth. Although the M&GN closed to passenger (Cromer-Melton Constable excepted) and general freight there was still a requirement for access to the former Norwich City station that had become a freight, terminal. Until the opening of the Themelthorpe curve mentioned earlier, trains had to run the 'long way round': Norwich Thorpe-Wroxham-the Cromer avoiding line-Sheringham-Melton Constable-Norwich City. The extensive sidings here were used for the stabling of carriage stock and wagon storage. Brush Type 2 No. D5533 arrives running light past a rake of what appears to be condemned rolling stock stored at Melton West junction. *Dr Ian C Allen.*

Opposite bottom: At the time of closure two Hunslet 204hp shunter locomotives, Nos. 11170 (later D2567) and 11176 (D2573) were shedded here; they acted as workshop and Norwich City pilots. On a later date Melton Constable locomotive shed's only occupant is a BR 204hp shunter. The shed was rebuilt in 1951, holding 12 locomotives it was in use for less than a decade; and with no other stock in view, the locomotive had probably arrived to power the track lifting trains. The general air of dereliction confirms the fact, that on 28th February 1959 most of the former M&GN was closed. Passenger services survived on the line from Sheringham to Melton Constable until the Beeching axe of 1964. *Dr Ian C Allen 106.*

Following closure to passenger services on 28th February 1959, the line from South Lynn to East Rudham remained open for freight traffic until May 1968. Here at Massingham the Guard has opened the level crossing gates as Brush Type 2 No. D5631 heads a short train from the Anglian Grain Co's depot at East Rudham. The yard here remained open for general freight until 1st January 1966. *Dr Ian C Allen D475.*

To the west of Massingham was Wilson's Siding, seen here with an unidentified BR 204hp shunter. The siding served Mr Wilson's stone quarry that provided a source of railway ballast from 1900 to 1914. The Air Ministry established a rail served depot here just before World War 2 – the fuel unloading gantries can be seen on the left. Trains of fuel ran from South Lynn to Massingham, the locomotive would run round before returning to the siding and propel the loaded tanks into the depot. *Dr Ian C Allen 255.*

Way out towards the western end of the M&GN, its line crossed that of the Great Northern & Great Eastern joint line between March and Spalding at Murrow. Unusually the crossing was on the level as can be seen in the illustrations. The GN&GE joint opened 2nd September 1867, and stopping passenger services ceased on 11th September 1961. Brush Type 4 No. D1759 heads north light engine. Upon closure of the M&GN a connecting line was laid to enable freight traffic to continue to serve Eye Green brick works as seen here. *Dr Ian C Allen 241.*

English Electric Type 4 No. D250 and train cross the by now closed M&GN route running south to March. The GN&GE joint line closed completely in 1982. *Dr Ian C Allen 066.*

Norfolk & Suffolk Joint

The N&SJt was owned by the GER and the M&GN, it consisted of two distinct sections: a line between North Walsham and Cromer via Mundesley, and a coastal section running from Gorleston to Lowestoft. Neither has survived apart from a short stretch just south of Cromer, connecting the GER and M&GN lines, that forms part of today's Bittern Line.

Above: The station at Paston & Knapton Halt has seen better days as a two-car Derby Lightweight unit heads north to Mundesley, by now the end of the line. The line between North Walsham junction to Mundesley was closed to passengers on 5th October 1964, with general freight traffic ending on 17th May 1965. *Dr Ian C Allen 113.*

Opposite: In an attempt to get more business, four GER bogie coaches were converted into Camping Coaches and stationed at Mundesley; eventually six were on site including ex-GNR No 2701 (LNER 42701, now numbered CC157), 3rd from the right in the lower image is now preserved on the Severn Valley Railway. It is believed to be the highest concentration of camping coaches in the country; however even they were not able to save the line from closure. The line northwards from Mundesley to Roughton Road Junction, just to the south of Cromer, had closed to all services on 7th April 1953. These two shots were probably taken on the same visit and show a Derby Lightweight unit operating the Mundesley-Norwich service. *Dr Ian C Allen 033 / 111.*

13

Norwich - Brandon

The Norwich & Brandon Railway was built from the end on junction with the Northern & Eastern Railway at Brandon, via Thetford and Wymondham to the Yarmouth & Norwich Railway to reach Norwich. It opened on 30th July 1845, but Norwich itself was not finally reached until 15th December 1845. The line was forced to terminate on the west side of the River Wensum pending completion of the swing bridge at Trowse.

Above: The Norfolk Railway opened Wymondham station on 30th July 1845. On 15th February 1847 it became a junction station with the opening of the Wymondham–Dereham–Wells line. Further expansion took place on 2nd May 1891 with the opening of the cut-off line via Ashwellthorpe to Forncett. The latter line closed to passengers on 10th September 1939, remaining open for general freight traffic until 4th August 1951. Wymondham coal yard was on the northern side of the station, with an unidentified BR 204hp shunter standing in the down bay platform. *Dr Ian C Allen 658.*

Opposite: On the upside, another 204hp shunter No. D2033 stands between duties behind the station building on the island platform. The main general goods yard was on this side of the station. *Dr Ian C Allen 224.*

Wymondham South Junction

A general view of Wymondham South Junction taken from the station footbridge. The Norwich-Thetford line runs through the centre of the image with the line to Dereham curving to the right of the signalbox. The scene is perhaps not as busy as it seems as the area was a concentration point for condemned coaching stock. The Cravens Class 105 DMU is Norwich-bound. *Dr Ian C Allen 402.*

As the shunters that operated here would have been allocated to Norwich for maintenance, they were generally attached to runner wagons to ensure any signalling track circuits would be activated. The shunters had regular trips along the short section of main line to the former Forncett branch as the former double tracked line was used as additional storage sidings for condemned stock. *Dr Ian C Allen 744.*

A parcels train hauled by Brush Type 2 No. D5566 passes the junction. The line immediately behind the signalbox once led to a turntable, now just a pit for servicing steam locomotives. The Mid-Norfolk Railway now operates the line to Dereham, although the junction here still exists and is used on a regular basis, passenger trains running from Wymondham Abbey station about a mile or so along the branch.
Dr Ian C Allen 202.

What appears to be BR 204hp shunter No. 2035, it was allocated to Norwich Thorpe at the time, is probably parked up for the weekend behind the signal box at South Junction. The line heading northwards to Dereham and Wells disappears off into the distance with a 30mph speed limit. The training tower for the fire station can be seen nestled amongst the trees. Although now part of the Mid-Norfolk Railway this section of line is only used to gain access to or from the heritage railway. *Dr Ian C Allen 1228.*

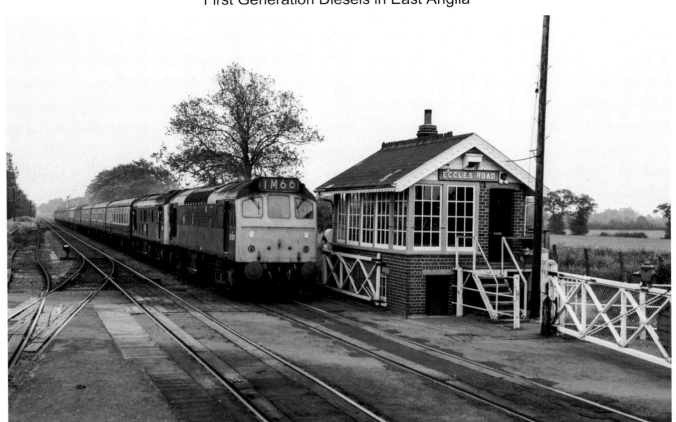

Opposite top: Double headed Type 2s, led by No. 7517, pass the signal box at Eccles Road on a southbound service. The station opened 30th July 1845, and closed to general freight traffic 18th April 1966, although a private siding remained operational for over two decades. As with other stations on the line the level crossing arrangements have since been modernised. *Dr Ian C Allen 387.*

Opposite bottom: A six-car Derby Lightweight set Norwich-bound at Harling Road. The road across the railway has since been upgraded; although the wooden level crossing gates adjacent to the station used to be opened and closed manually by a signaller in the signal box. It was not until December 2012 that the signal box was closed and the crossing was renewed with automatic barriers and warning lights. *Dr Ian C Allen 715.*

This page: A BR 204hp shunter making the long journey to Norwich is seen at Roundham Junction, the station here closed on 1st May 1932; although it remained open unofficially as a request stop until complete closure of the Swaffham branch. The line curving away to the left of the signalbox was the line to Swaffham via Watton. Opened as far north as Watton on 18th October 1869, the section from there to Swaffham opened on 15th November 1875. The section south of Watton closed to all traffic on 15th June 1964; the northern section retained freight services until 1965. *Dr Ian C Allen 061.*

Top: English Electric Type 3 No. D6702 runs east bound past Thetford signalbox with a mixed freight train in tow. There is still an extensive coal trade as evidenced by the coal yard. Thetford was the junction for a line south to Bury St. Edmunds. Opening to passenger traffic on 1st March 1876, the service lasted until 8th June 1953. Final closure to freight came in 1960. No. D6702 was delivered to BR in December 1960 and survived for almost 40 years. *Dr Ian C Allen 031.*

Left and opposite top: At Two Mile Bottom between Thetford and Brandon was a private siding that served the Fison's Fertiliser Factory. The manure works was first built in 1853, with production ceasing in 1954. The site was then used as storage before being demolished in 1975. The private siding allowed for coal deliveries as the plant was initially steam driven. The factory was updated in 1921 with Ruston & Hornsby oil engines. Later in 1937 their horse drawn wagons were replaced by tractors. A two-car Metropolitan-Cammell set heads towards Cambridge. Whilst Brush Type 2 No. D5814 stands at the head of a lengthy northbound freight. For weather watchers Santon Downham is nearby, often recorded as the coldest place in England.
Dr Ian C Allen 049 / 1214.

Right: Returning briefly to Roundham Junction, which incidentally closed to passengers on 1st May 1932, there was a line heading towards Swaffam. Brush Type 2 No. D5559 draws a single box van and brake into the station at Holme Hale. Track rationalisation has taken place with the entry to the passing loop taken out.
Dr Ian C Allen 1035.

14

Wymondham - Wells

The Norfolk Railway (NR) was formed by an amalgamation of the Norwich & Bandon and Yarmouth & Norwich railways. The NR opened the section from Wymondham to Dereham on 15th February 1847, extending to Fakenham on 20th March 1849. The NR was leased to the Eastern Counties Railway on 8th May 1848, later becoming part of the GER. The Wells & Fakenham Railway opened the section north from Fakenham, via Walsingham, on 1st December 1857. Worked by the ECR, it became part of the GER on 7th August 1892.

BR 204hp shunter No. D2034 has arrived light engine at Hardingham from the Dereham direction. As part of the rationalisation programme the branch was singled in June 1968 although the former double track formation can be seen. Hardingham was retained as a passing loop until passenger services ended in October 1969. There were several sidings in the goods yard, other facilities included a rail-connected granary and cattle dock; however, unlike some other stations on the line general freight services ceased on 18th April 1966. *Dr Ian C Allen 942.*

Dereham

Top: With the signal box proudly bearing Dereham Central, the signalman has obtained the single line token from the driver as this Metropolitan-Cammell unit arrives at Dereham on its way to King's Lynn. The station was built in stages, being expanded over several decades. It was provided with four platforms, platforms 2 and 3 being set back to back. Platform 4 was a short bay platform and was originally dedicated for trains heading towards King's Lynn.
Dr Ian C Allen 068.

Centre: With Dr Allen having gained a higher vantage point in the signal box, he photographed the unit as it continued its journey westward to King's Lynn. With lines heading north, south and west, four signal boxes controlled Dereham, with Central handling the main station area. There was a south to west curve enabling freight traffic to have a direct route. Freight traffic at the station included the gas works, maltings, fertilizer and various agricultural premises. It was not unknown for services terminating at Dereham to have the unit stabled in the engine shed overnight.
Dr Ian C Allen 277.

Bottom: By now sporting a full yellow cab and the 'arrows of indecision', this blue painted unit runs in from King's Lynn, to reverse and continue to Norwich. The station was closed to passengers on 6th October 1969. Remaining open for coal traffic until 12th September 1984, although freight services continued to North Elmham until 1989. Today the line through Dereham and south to Wymondham operates as the Mid-Norfolk Railway. Plans are in place to reopen to County School.
Dr Ian C Allen 122.

Top: The second station north from Dereham was County School, just south of the junction for the Reepham-Aylsham-Wroxham line. This was an isolated rural station, indeed if it was not for the signpost reading County School Station, most people would not know it existed. It did, however, serve the Norfolk County School, a few hundred yards away. Later the school became 'The Watts Naval Training School', a branch of Dr Barnardo's Homes. Otherwise it only served scattered farms and cottages. A two-car Metropolitan-Cammell unit operates a Wells-Norwich service. *Dr Ian C Allen 1084.*

Bottom: Fakenham East was the principal station with a passenger crossing loop between County School and Wells. The adjacent granary was a source of traffic for the railway. The DMU is exiting the passenger-crossing loop before arriving at the single platform, as with the rest of the line north of Dereham, closure to passengers came on 5th October 1964; freight traffic survived until 1st January 1980. In this view Brush Type 2 No. D5559 hides in the shadows whilst engaged in shunting the yard. *Dr Ian C Allen 267.*

Top and centre: On 21st April 1979 the Wymondham, Dereham & Fakenham Railway Action Committee ran the 'Fakenham Flyer' from Norwich to Fakenham over the freight only line; but later that year it was announced that the section of line between Ryburgh and Fakenham would close from 1st January 1980. Before this however, the site was rationalised and Brush Type 2 No. D5545 is amongst the action as the demolition teams move in. Following closure it was general practise to remove the infrastructure for recycling. Initially this was carried out using direct labour, later being contracted out as BR had fewer men on the ground. Viewed from the road bridge seen in the previous image it will not take long to clear the station site, just leaving limited track for the surviving freight traffic.
Dr Ian C Allen 189 / 453.

Bottom: Brush Type 2 No. D5554 prepares to head south with reclaimed material for recycling. Following rationalisation a line was left to serve the platform with a single line crossing the road to access the maltings seen above the train. The maltings closed towards the end of the 20th Century and a care home now occupies the site. *Dr Ian C Allen 082.*

Wells-next-the-Sea was the northern terminus of the line from Wymondham. Opening on 1st December 1857 as Wells, renaming came on 1st July 1923 to Wells-on-Sea, then again on 1st January 1957 to the name the town still retains. The next line to arrive in Wells was the West Norfolk Junction Railway's line from Heacham. The latter's stations were inconveniently located; passenger services were withdrawn on 2nd June 1952, the line remaining open for freight traffic for a further few years. Services continued south to Dereham until 5th October 1964. The fixed distant (top signal on the post) protects the level crossing over the A149 just to the south of Wells-next-the-Sea as a Metropolitan-Cammell unit heads towards Dereham, Wymondham and Norwich. Immediately to the south of the crossing is the northern terminus of the 10¼in gauge Wells & Walsingham Railway. *Dr Ian C Allen D763.*

15

King's Lynn - Dereham

The Lynn & Dereham Railway was authorized to build a line between the two towns named. The first section, Lynn to Narborough, opened on 27th October 1846.

The company was then acquired by the East Anglian Railways. Opening to Dereham was on 11th September 1848. It became part of the GER in 1862.

Middleton station was the first stopping place on the route from Lynn to Swaffham and Dereham.
The village of Middleton is more than a mile to the south of the station that bore its name. A small hamlet known as Tower End is nearer and accounts for the name later adopted for the station from 1924.
The short section of track between King's Lynn and Middleton Towers remains open for freight traffic.
The local sand being much prized for use in the glass industry. Here Brush Type 2 No. D5581 is departing for King's Lynn; it has acquired a yellow front end to aid visibility for line-side workers. *Dr Ian C Allen 070.*

Brush Type 2 No. D5581 in the midst of the action at Middleton Towers. The locomotive standing by the sign dating from LNER days is British Industrial Sand Ltd's Motor Rail, works No. 4218 dating from 1933. As well as the standard gauge line, the sand pits were worked by a 2ft gauge network. In the early 1970s seven locomotives worked on the pit lines, today conveyer-belts transport the sand to the loaders. *Dr Ian C Allen 420.*

Dunham station following rationalisation; its name had already been shortened, opening as Little Dunham on 11th September 1848; it was renamed Dunham in September 1851. The track layout was reduced to a single line through the station in the summer of 1964 and 'pay train' operation meant that there was no station staff. The two car Metropolitan-Cammell Lightweight DMU is operating a King's Lynn-Dereham-Norwich service. Beeching's report into the modernisation of Britain's railways expected the line to remain open, but closure came on 9th September 1968. *Dr Ian C Allen 008.*

King's Lynn - Hunstanton

Construction of the King's Lynn–Hunstanton line coincided with the rising popularity of northwest Norfolk as a destination for holidaymakers who were arriving in large numbers. Hunstanton was promoted as a seaside resort by Henry Styleman Le Strange (1815-1862), lord of the manor and principal landowner, who gifted land and money towards the line's construction. Although the line was not listed for closure in the Beeching report, freight services were withdrawn in 1964, and the line reduced to 'basic railway' standard that was completed during 1967.

Top: Probably one of the most recognisable stations in Norfolk is Wolferton. Despite having one of the smallest parish populations at the time of its opening it enjoyed a disproportionate amount of fame, being the local station to the Sandringham Estate. Opening on 3rd October 1862, the station was enlarged from a single to the double platform as seen here. The two-car Gloucester unit awaits departure for King's Lynn following rationalisation of the route. *Dr Ian C Allen 711.*

Right: As with many routes in East Anglia this was an early closure – passenger traffic from Heacham to Wells-next-the-Sea ceasing on 31st May 1952. However, a daily goods service remained and in the early 1960s Brush Type 2 No. D5617 is seen at Burnham Market. The crew would shunt the intermediate stations of Sedgford and Docking during the round trip. The section between here and Wells was a victim of the January 1953 flooding, repair not being viable for one freight train a day. *Dr Ian C Allen D388.*

South of King's Lynn

The line, south from King's Lynn, was opened by the Lynn & Ely Railway as far as Downham Market on 29th October 1846. Following a series of amalgamations the line to Ely opened on 26th October 1847. The line to Wisbech was opened from Magdalen Gate junction to the town on 2nd February 1848.

To Wisbech (& Upwell)

Above: Silhouetted against the evening sky, a two-car DMU crosses the bridge over the River Ouse, just to the east of short-lived Magdalen Gate station. The station opened on 1st March 1848, closing on 1st August 1866. *Dr Ian C Allen 419.*

Opposite top: Middle Drove station served the village of Tilney Fen End, near Downham Market. The station was opened on 1st March 1848 as an extension of the East Anglian Railway's line from Magdalen Road (now known as Watlington) station to Wisbech East. The station's location, like that of the neighbouring Smeeth Road station, was fairly rural and the line eventually closed on 9th September 1968. A two-car Derby Lightweight unit departs Middle Drove bound for Wisbech. *Dr Ian C Allen 131.*

Opposite bottom: Emneth, as Brush Type 2 No. D5573 rolls out of the station past the signal box with a three-coach train on its way to Wisbech. Note the driver reaching out to collect the token that will allow access to the single line section. Today Emneth is best known as being the home of the late Rev Wilbert Awdry – author of the 'Thomas the Tank engine' series of books. *Dr Ian C Allen 250.*

Taken from the other side of the signal box, this view shows the mix of upper and lower quadrant signals at Emneth. With the destination screen on the rear of this Derby Lightweight unit showing the journey's end, it departs for Wisbech East. *Dr Ian C Allen 472.*

Wisbech & Upwell Tramway.

Following the withdrawal of the steam tram locomotives that operated over the rural, but busy during picking season, tramway, Drewry shunter diesels were in full control. The locomotives that operated on the Wisbech & Upwell line had to be fitted with cow-catchers, side-skirts and speed governors to be able to work the roadside tramway. Here the crew of Drewry No. D2202, along with the guard, appear to be enjoying their day out! *Dr Ian C Allen 541.*

No. D2202 crosses the Village Bridge at the entrance to Upwell Village Depot. Many farms on the fens were only accessible by water until well into the 20th Century. With around 40 pumping stations keeping the land above water level, a Fenland Lighter from Outwell Basin depot supplied them with coal. *Dr Ian C Allen 1233.*

With the tower and spire of St Clement's Church in the background, No. D2202 leaves Outwell for Upwell. The church, sited at the centre of Outwell village in the Fens on the Norfolk-Cambridgeshire border, is a treasure house of unique mediaeval sculptures and beautiful stained glass.
Dr Ian C Allen 1231.

Above: An out of the fruit season image at Upwell Depot. The Drewry shunter has arrived with some mineral wagons loaded with coal and is arranging the empties for return to the collieries.
Dr Ian C Allen 1267.

Opposite top: Returning to the main line south from King's Lynn, we arrive at Black Drove where Brush Type 2 No. D5622 heads south. The actual location is named Black Horse Drove and is located between Hilgay station (opened with the line on 25th October 1847, and closing on 4th November 1963), and Littleport. *Dr Ian C Allen 266.*

Opposite bottom: The Eastern Counties Railway opened Ely station on 30th July, the land on which it was built being a marshy swamp. At the centre of five converging routes it remains busy and was modified substantially in the early 1990s, at the time that electrification of the King's Lynn line was taking place. Long before electrification was considered, a two-car Metropolitan-Cammell lightweight unit heads north to King's Lynn. The Ruston shunter stands at the entrance to the private sidings of G G Papworth, which is still in operation today as the Ely Freight Terminal. *Dr Ian C Allen 043.*

18

Stoke Ferry Branch

The Stoke Ferry line started life as so many in East Anglia; missed by the main lines, many places wanted a connection to the outside world so that they did not miss out on the trade and prosperity.

The Downham & Stoke Ferry Railway opened the line on 1st August 1882. What made this line of interest was the connection to the Wissington industrial network that served the sugar beet industry. The Wissington Railway itself closed on 30th June 1957, leaving a short stub that remained open as a private siding servicing the factory. Sugar beet traffic continued until well after closure of the branch to all other traffic.

Brush Type 2 No. D5528 stands in the platform at Abbey & West Dereham station which remains remarkably intact. Opened as Abbey on 1st August 1882, the station was renamed Abbey for West Dereham on 1st January 1866, finally becoming Abbey & West Dereham on 1st July 1923. The line closed to passengers on 22nd September 1930. Someone is putting the line-side to good use as an allotment; and the flatness of the fens can be appreciated. *Dr Ian C Allen 675.*

Another Brush Type 2, this time No. D5581, is seen at the exchange sidings that were at the east end of Abbey & West Dereham station. Once the line had closed to passenger and general freight traffic, this became the end of the line for main line locomotives. Inbound sugar beet traffic came to an end in 1975 when the British Sugar Corporation made the decision to end beet traffic by rail. *Dr Ian C Allen 094.*

Brush Type 2 No. D5666 and Fowler 0-4-0DH (works No. 4220033/1965) at the exchange sidings at Abbey. The sign to the right of the Fowler reads 'No engine to pass this board'; obviously this only applies to main line locomotives. During the crushing season, coal and limestone traffic continued to be delivered. Outbound traffic consisted of refined sugar, pulp nuts and molasses. *Dr Ian C Allen 406.*

An unidentified Brush Type 2 stands at the literal end of the line at Stoke Ferry, 7¼ miles from Denver. The second man looks back, perhaps to ensure the photographer has got his shot, before the engine runs round and shunts a short freight that appears to consist of just a box and brake van. The section of line between Abbey and Stoke Ferry closed to general freight traffic in 1965. *Dr Ian C Allen 256.*

19

The End

Along with the closure of much of the rail network in Norfolk and Suffolk during the 1950s and 1960s, vast amounts of locomotives and rolling stock was surplus to requirements. Although there was no steel works in the area the firm, of A King & Sons Ltd, or Norwich, was active in the recycling of redundant assets.

Opposite top: The firm of A King & Sons of Norwich was responsible for scrapping around 100 steam locomotives towards the end of steam. The firm then turned to diesels; withdrawn from Scottish depots in 1971, 11 Clayton Type 1 (Class 17) Bo-Bo diesels were dragged south to Norwich. Seen here stored at Trowse prior to dismantling is No. D8531 together with other members of the class.
Dr Ian C Allen 398.

Opposite bottom: With the closed line between Wymondham and Forncett available, BR used it for the storage of redundant rolling stock awaiting recycling. Even the prestigious Pullman Cars were not safe; here No. D2018 shunts three such vehicles. Immediately behind the 204hp shunter is 'Daisy', a Parlour Car with Kitchen, it was formed in Southern Railway '6PUL' unit No. 2010 (later 3010) from 1932 until withdrawal in 1965. *Dr Ian C Allen 511.*

This page, top: Kings had a second yard at Snailwell where coaching stock was recycled. With a large quantity of worthless, at least as far as a scrap merchant was concerned, material therein, a quick and easy way was required to dispose of the coaches as efficiently as possible. In consequence Kings built an incinerator at Snailwell, near Newmarket. Complete coaches were pushed in one end, burnt of all combustible material and the metal remains cut for scrap. The results can be seen here with numerous coach underframes awaiting recycling. The yard is still operational as part of the EMR Group.
Dr Ian C Allen 538.

Towards the end of the 1940s the Great Western ordered two gas turbine locomotives. The first of these was numbered 18000 and delivered by Brown-Boveri of Switzerland in 1949. It was withdrawn in 1960 and later passed to the International Union of Railways in Switzerland. It is seen here being hauled to Harwich docks by Brush Type 2 No. D5666. As a shell and minus its turbine, No. 18000 was returned to the UK for preservation in January 1994. No. D5666 was withdrawn in August 1999 by now as No. 31439 but it was not finally cut up until 2010/11. *Dr Ian C Allen 997.*

Bibliography / Further reading

The following are just a selection of books that have been referred to during the writing of this book:

Brodribb, J.; *Branches & Byways: East Anglia*, 9780860935490, OPC, 2000.
Brodribb, J.; *The Main Lines of East Anglia*, 9780860936299, OPC, 2009.
Brodribb, J.; *First Generation DMUs in East Anglia*, 9780711031395, Ian Allan, 2006.
Butlin, A.; *Diesel & Electric Locomotives for Scrap*, 9780860936701, OPC, 2015.
Butt, R. V. J.; *The Directory of Railway Stations*, 9781852605087, PSL, 1995.
Cobb, M. H.; *The Railways of Great Britain: A Historical Atlas* (2nd Edn), 071103236X, Ian Allan Publishing, 2006.
Digby, N. J. L.; *The Stations and Structures of the Midland & Great Northern Joint Railway: Vol 1 Lowestoft to Melton Constable*, 9781899889822, Lightmoor, 2014.
Digby, N. J. L.; *The Stations and Structures of the Midland & Great Northern Joint Railway: Vol 2 Norwich to Peterborough and Little Bytham*, 9781911030816, Lightmoor, 2015.
Ford, A. M.; *Pullman Profile No 4*, 9781909328051, Noodle Books, 2012.
Gammell, C. J.; *LNER Branch Lines*, 9780860935094, OPC, 1993.
Gordon, D. I.; *A Regional History of the Railways of Great Britain: Volume 5 The Eastern Counties*, 0715374311, David & Charles.
Green-Hughes, E.; BT *First Generation Diesel Railbuses*, 9780711036352, Ian Allan, 2011.
Grant, D. J.; *Directory of the Railway Companies of Great Britain*, 9781788037686, Matador, 2017.
Hawkins, C.; *Great Eastern in Town & Country: Vol 1*, 9780871608168, Irwell Press, 1990.
Hawkins, C.; *Great Eastern in Town & Country: Vol 2*, 9780871608250, Irwell Press, 1991.
Hawkins, C. & Reeve, G.; *Great Eastern Railway Engine Sheds: Vol 1*, 0906867401, Wild Swan, 1986.
Hawkins, C. & Reeve, G.; *Great Eastern Railway Engine Sheds: Vol 2*, 0906867487, Wild Swan, 1987.
Jenkins, S. C.; *The Cromer Branch*, 0853613842, Oakwood, 1989.
Jenkins, S. C.; *The Lynn and Dereham Railway*, 0853614421, Oakwood, 1993.
Jenkins, S. C.; *The Lynn and Hunstanton Railway and the West Norfolk Branch*, 08536133303, Oakwood, 1987.
Jenkins, S. C.; *The Wells-next-the Sea Branch, via Wymondham and Dereham*, 0853613745, Oakwood, 1988.
Kay, P.; *Great Eastern in Town & Country: Vol 3*, 9780871608748, Irwell Press, 1996.
Marsden, C. J.; *DMU and EMU Recognition Guide*, 9780711037403, Ian Allan Publishing, 2013.

Middleton Press publish numerous titles in its 'Branch Lines Around', Branch' Lines to', 'Country Railway Routes' series.

There were several stations in Wisbech plus associated changes of name. An early example of the latter, on 4th May 1877, was the change of railway spelling from Wisbeach. For the full story *Branch Lines Around Wisbech* is recommended. As far as our journey is concerned Wisbech East passenger station is also our final destination. Drewry 204hp shunter No. D2201 standing alongside the island platform at Wisbech East. It would, on Friday, 20th May 1966, work the last tram through the station from Upwell.
Dr Ian C Allen 1148.